SUCCESS IS...

Principles for Achieving Your Dreams

By
Peter J. Daniels

Aircrew Member of The Year (SNCO)
SMSgt Benjamin Van Vleet (2001)

Trade Life Books
Tulsa, Oklahoma

2nd Printing

Success Is...
— *Principles for Achieving Your Dreams*
ISBN 1-57757-036-7
Copyright © 1998 by Peter J. Daniels
38-40 Carrington Street
Adelaide, South Australia, Australia 5000

Published by Trade Life Books
P. O. Box 55325
Tulsa, Oklahoma 74155

Printed in the United States of America. All rights reserved under International Copyright Law. Contents and/or cover may not be reproduced in whole or in part in any form without the express written consent of the Publisher.

Introduction

This book is the distilled essence of my life's experience, as a husband married for 44 years, as a father of three dynamic and committed adult children, and as a grandfather of eight grandchildren who think I am the fourth member of the Trinity.

My direct involvement on the cutting edge of business throughout the world, together with my deep commitment to biblical values and political connections, has provided a kaleidoscope view of difficulties, innuendoes, hair-splitting, and just plain folly in the parade of life.

Most of the contents of this book are from my own experience, but some are keys I have picked up along the way because they worked for other successful people. I trust that when difficulties arise or uncertainty causes a question about which move you should make, this book will provide the answer. Read and re-read the principles contained in these pages and make them part of your vocabulary. I am confident you will benefit from them and thus live a more productive and peaceful life.

Success Is...

Success is acceptance of
yourself.

Appreciating your position in life and not wallowing in despair of your misfortunes and lack of talent is the first step toward leading a successful and productive life. You can rise above everything if you believe in yourself.

Success Is...

Success is having consistent
work habits.

Make a routine of listing all necessary requirements to complete your given task and leave plenty of time for dreaming, negotiating, and grasping new opportunities. One of the great keys of success is to develop habit-force, which means that many essentials are just done by good habit procedure.

Success Is...

Success is having the resilience
to rise again from defeat.

Some people stay in the timid waters of mediocrity because they have had one or two failures. If you study the lives of successful people, you will find that many of them failed several times before finally gaining success, and so can you.

Success Is...

Success is not blaming other people for your problems.

Accepting responsibility for your own actions and for your own problems is the first sign of a healthy mind. Take care, for the insignificant person inside of you has the potential to achieve greatness.

Success Is...

Success is understanding that time is your most valuable possession.

Time is the stuff that life is made of. You can always make more money, but you cannot make one more moment of time. Take time out to play, to be with your family, and to enjoy life. Waste not one moment of it — it is irreplaceable.

Success Is...

Success is learning to speak on your feet coherently.

You may only get one or two major opportunities in your life to address a large crowd or a major television audience. Remember the words of Abraham Lincoln, "I will study, I will prepare, and my opportunity will come." You should practice, practice, practice public speaking until you perfect it and can speak confidently anywhere, at any time, under any circumstance. It will be one of your greatest assets.

Success Is...

Success is created by
recognizing, accepting, and
using worthy opportunities to
their fullest extent.

Many people do not recognize opportunities when they are presented to them and if they do, they respond tentatively, not fully developing those opportunities. To be successful means using every attribute, to the fullest, that you possess.

Success Is...

Success is understanding that procrastination is trying to avoid life.

Mastery over procrastination is the first tool of leadership, whether it be economic, spiritual, or military. When there is nothing to lose by trying and everything to gain, by all means try! Procrastination is full of regrets and good intentions. Conquer it and you will out-distance all else.

Success Is...

Success is understanding
there is nothing as permanent
as change.

All records will be broken, all limits will be surpassed, all normalities will be extended. This is called progress. People will always push themselves to the heights of their dreams and aspirations — and so can you!

Success Is...

Success is understanding that every mistake has its own penalty.

Some people go through life making repetitive mistakes and wonder why, at the end of their life, they have not made their mark on the world or achieved success. Learning from mistakes is smart.

Success Is...

Success is understanding that
life is choices, not chances.

Bad choices produce a bad lifestyle and failure. Look at your past choices and ask yourself, "Had I made a different choice, would I be better off today?" The answer will probably be "Yes."

Success Is...

Success is understanding that invariably truth is the first casualty in all conflicts, but in the end its incorruptible force will stand supreme.

Truth is incontrovertible. It can stand up to all onslaughts and criticism, and will rise supreme at every conflict.

Success Is...

Success is having the power to absorb information.

Many people go through a lifetime saying they cannot read, they cannot remember, and they cannot absorb. But information is very similar to physical fitness. If you were to begin doing push-ups, you may only be able to do a few. However, with practice you would gain strength. The mind is like a muscle and can be developed. Regular reading brushes away the cobwebs and develops the mind.

Success Is...

Success is understanding that without a vigorous spirit, the dream will not come to fruition.

Look around you, and you will find many people with similar attributes but only one will stand alone because of the spirit within. This dynamic spirit can be developed because of a dream, and when that dream is passed on to a clear vision that can be seen, and you are prepared to trade your life for it, the dynamics in your spirit will respond.

Success Is...

Success is having an
urgency factor.

Most people get along by going along. Realize that opportunities are often like slippery fish — they can slip out of your hands and be gone forever. An urgency factor is necessary to succeed, to grasp the opportunity at hand, and to make the most of it.

Success is focusing on one
single target for victory.

Many people try to succeed by doing several things at once. They work on one project, only partially committed, and then they try to do something else that is alien to the original concept. If you want to succeed, give one thing everything you've got — and then some.

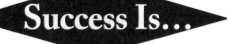
Success Is...

Success is adopting priority economics.

Do things in order of their importance, not in order of demand. Concentrate on that which responds to your economic future rather than that which can be wasted and squandered. Too often work is programmed toward fantasy rather than reality.

Success Is...

Success is understanding that
your darkest hour may have
within it your brightest hope.

Success is often lost because defeat is accepted much too early. Yet, even in defeat, if you face it with a positive mental attitude, full of optimism and hope, you may see a new light that will lead to far greener pastures — and even be better than what you had hoped for.

Success Is...

Success is understanding that motivation always comes with a sense of the future.

Talking about and regurgitating the past rarely helps the future. You can always identify people who have lost their hope. They are always discussing what could have been or what was. Success is a growing thing in the now and the future.

Success Is...

Success is understanding how much of yourself you are prepared to give.

Productivity is inseparably tied to purity. Be honest with yourself, dedicated to the task at hand, and give it everything you've got. Withholding your best or reluctance in performance will never seize the prize.

Success Is...

Success is creating checkpoints
that are realistic.

Have dates, times, and measurements for achievement as checkpoints to know how far you've come and how far you have to go. Without that, you are merely playing games with hope, but without facts.

Success Is...

Success is understanding that theorists suggest and pragmatists do.

I have met people in all walks of life who put things on paper, suggest what they are going to do, write great plans, and talk philosophy, but they never get from the paper to the road. Be a pragmatist and get things done.

Success Is...

Success is understanding that
good morals is good economics.

Telling the truth, keeping your word, producing a good product, rendering good service, and obeying the laws of God and man is good economics. The good guys really do win.

Success Is...

Success is responding to failure
and crisis with optimism.

Failure and success in life are better than
a university education. And, if you
document your failures and your successes,
and reverse your failure decisions,
you will have success with optimism.

Success Is...

Success is having confidence in your ability to adjust and win in the midst of changing circumstances.

The Asian world gives a double meaning to the word "crisis" — danger and opportunity. Within every crisis is an opportunity. The bigger the crisis, the bigger the opportunity. Most people are too fearful to enter through its doors and grasp what is waiting for them.

Success Is...

Success is knowing what your
inner belief will permit you
to do.

Go sit at the seashore and think of what your inner beliefs will permit you to do. Don't wait until difficulties descend upon you to debate what you are prepared to trade your life for.

Success Is...

Success is having a short-term
view when assessing
performance and a long-term
view when assessing success.

Performance must be measured on a daily basis and then rechecked weekly and monthly. You will find the road to success is achieved by measured progress.

Success Is...

Success is reaching your final destination with clear, measurable, specific, and quality results.

By all means look ahead to the final goal, but then tackle the task in bite sized chunks with measurements, specifics, time, quality, and quantitative values. Unless you do this, putting it on paper in these increments, success will evade you.

Success is having people assist you who possess strengths you lack. They fill in the gaps.

No person, however brilliant, has all the necessary qualities for success in their chosen field. You must rely on other people and learn the "people" business. Find out what their dreams are and see if you can help them reach their dream by fulfilling yours.

Success Is...

Success is not being threatened
by others.

Some people waste a lot of time trying to outmaneuver others, placing obstacles in their way and whispering behind their backs. In the long run, the easiest and most beneficial thing to do is to out-distance everyone else.

Success Is...

Success is understanding that
any fool can beat mediocrity.

Average is not for the high achiever and should not be part of their vocabulary. The world would abruptly stop if we had average doctors, average engineers, and average airplane mechanics. Always try to be the best you can possibly be, then beat it.

Success Is...

Success is understanding that there is nothing more hazardous to your health than poverty.

Disappointment, heartbreak, overwork, and worry over finances create ulcers, heart attacks, and all kinds of illnesses. With sufficient income, you can rise above most of these and live a fruitful and productive life.

Success Is...

Success is understanding that economics does not start with goods; it starts with people.

Most people are waiting for finances, products, or unusual opportunities to come knocking on their door. Prosperity does not come this way. It is sought out by individuals who develop an idea, chase a dream, and inspire others.

Success Is...

Success is understanding that
life is attitude.

Attitude is more important than facts, more important than positioning, and more relevant than circumstances. With the right attitude — even in the wrong situation — all will be well. Always look at difficulties with a positive expectancy — seeking, expecting, and striving for the best to come out of every situation. Develop an inspirational dissatisfaction.

Success Is...

Success is understanding that you either read or get out of business.

Military history will teach you tactics and courage. Biographies will develop your dreams and aspirations. Working on the highways and byways of life, being involved in the marketplace, and reading the signs of events will put you light-years in front of your competitors.

Success is understanding that
worry creates mental pictures
of the things you do not want.

Worry dries up your spirit and binds the imagination. It can change nothing, do nothing, and its value is zero. Stop now, become more creative, and your spirit will be lifted.

Success Is...

Success is making decisions
quickly and changing them
rarely.

When you do not make a decision you have, in a sense, decided not to decide and have left everything to circumstance. It is a convenient way to place blame for failures on the breaks of life, but it is not practical for a person seeking success.

Success Is...

Success is placing an extremely
high value on a lifetime.

Why not put a monetary value on your energy, your dreams, your brain power, and your heritage? If you were to add it all up, you would find the financial amount would be extravagant. Yet, you treat your life so casually and sell it for a pittance. Why not change and accept your own valuation report?

Success Is...

Success is understanding that
high achievers plan long and
keep short accounts with their
own ability.

Monitoring and comparing your ability with last year, five years, and ten years ago will give you an idea of how you have progressed or remained dormant. Write your abilities down regularly, assess them without pseudo-rationale, and monitor your own achievement quotient.

Success Is...

Success is understanding that
goal setting is a logical, fulfilling
approach to dynamic living.

Why not prepare your life as if you were taking a long journey?

1. Create a map to reach your goals.
2. Make a list of the equipment you need.
3. Carry a reminder card to keep you on track.

If you want something tomorrow, you must plan something today.

Success is understanding that
when others set your goals,
it destroys your personal
accountability.

Do not be a slave to someone else's predications or programs. It is your life. You are responsible for it and must not be manipulated by people or events.
Be accountable and set your own goals.
Watch out for having goals that conflict with one another.

Success Is...

Success is understanding that
we can all overcome rejection
and become stronger in spite
of it.

Never allow anyone to presume against you and make predictions about your life. A rejection against you is another person's opinion. Even IQ tests only tell you where you are – they don't tell you how far you can go.

Success Is...

Success is understanding that
you are the carrier of dreams,
dreams you are responsible
to fulfill.

Dreams don't work unless you do. The dreams you have must not be dependent upon someone else but must be fully dependent upon you. Do not expect others to subsidize your dream or pave the way for your dreams to come true. If God gave *you* the dream, He meant for *you* to pursue it.

Success Is...

Success is realizing that discipline will dispel fear and timidity.

Even mediocre talent and ability can be harnessed together with discipline. Geniuses fall by the wayside because of the lack of it. Great heroes and achievers, past and present, have held discipline high on the altar of achievement.

Success Is...

Success is not allowing others
to control you by their
predictions.

All leaders actually or potentially have power, but not all those with power are leaders. If you allow people to control you, you are relinquishing your God-given freedom of choice.

Success Is...

Success is the willingness to
bear pain.

I said, *bear* pain, not be a pain!
Understand that pain is weakness
escaping. Everyone has the ability to *bear*
pain, but do they have the willingness to
endure it for a higher benefit?

Success Is...

Success is believing that anything can be done by somebody. Why not you?

There is not a person, living or dead, that has every attribute for success. You are as well-equipped as anyone else. Stop asking why someone else has achieved, and ask yourself the question, "Why not me?" Then be prepared to pay the price. You will be surprised at how you will grow to meet the challenge.

Success Is...

Success is being in the position to help and influence others in a positive way because of your achievements.

Some people spend their lives trying to help others while forgetting to help themselves. You are a better help to others when you have achieved, because you know how to help people. You know what works and what does not. Scrutinize your own life first, make your own life a success, and *then* pass your wisdom on to others.

Success Is...

Success is understanding that
lack of education does not
prevent you from success —
lack of vision does.

Many people of low or modest education have risen above their circumstances and achieved remarkable success. The reason is they were visionaries. They saw what other people could not see and could not understand. Be a visionary and achieve greatness. The human spirit defies limitations.

Success Is...

Success is understanding that
negativity always binds the
receiver and gives control
to the sender.

Don't spend unnecessary time thinking about and dissecting negative comments. Once a negative comment is given by the sender, they generally forget about it, while the receiver is bound by the negativity.
Break the chains and ignore negativity.

Success Is...

Success is understanding that
fear kills confidence.

The path of failure is filled with fear, yet you cannot produce one ounce of it for the eye to see or the hand to touch. Treat fear as a challenge! Combat it with every ounce of strength you have, and you will find that it will flee from you.

Success Is...

Success is having confidence as
a result of over-preparing.

By preparing more than you need, you will have the mental and factual reserves to combat anything that is thrust upon you. It will also tell those you are dealing with that you are a serious and worthy contender.

Always under-commit and over-perform.

Success Is...

Success is understanding that a strong ego is not wrong, but a weak ego or an ego out of control is wrong.

The ego is part of the personality and the human psyche. It is not meant to be crushed; it is meant to be redeemed. If it is harnessed with two indispensable principles – truth and ability – it can be a powerful force for achievement and good.

Success Is...

Success is understanding that stress and pressure test your ethics.

Problems are always magnified under pressure. Retaining your dignity in difficult situations illustrates who you are and what real abilities you have. It is easy to be ethical while things are running smoothly, but when the heat is on, a person's real integrity is tested.

Success Is...

Success is never accepting that you are in a non-negotiating situation.

If you use your imagination and keep a positive mental attitude, you can develop a power position in any situation — even if it seems hopeless. Be creative, suggest options, and realize that every small problem you solve reduces the whole. Be innovative in your thinking and remind yourself that time can be your best or worst component.

Success Is...

Success is being careful of advice received from family or friends who do not understand the climate and the complexities of a difficult situation.

When acting upon advice given by others, evaluate the success they have had in their own lives and what advantage or disadvantage they have in giving you information. All too often we accept advice from people who love us, whether the advice is beneficial or not.

Success Is...

Success is understanding that nobody can get into your mind and body and act it out for you.

Relationships with successful people and great motivators can give you inspiration, but nobody can do for you what you can already do for yourself. Don't expect others to baby-sit you or nurse you. Make your own way in life.

Success Is...

Success is writing the worst known facts and fears of a difficult situation down on paper and then taking control of them.

Too often we allow rumors, perceptions, hearsay, and possibilities to bind us in a difficult situation. Always look at the facts, dissect them, and test them. Then cut the fetters from your mind, allowing it to glide as it is divinely designed to do.

Success Is...

Success is not confusing activity
with productivity.

We can go into a busy office and see people diligently working, others taking bulging briefcases home with them, some making business calls from their cars, and many hurrying to meet deadlines. But remember: all that really counts is results. Get the job done, and do not be persuaded or intimidated with too much activity – which can often be a smoke screen for confusion.

Success Is...

Success is understanding the only real measure of value is permanence.

All of us should leave a heritage for those coming after us. Most of our goals are in ten- or twenty-year terms, when in fact we could do something that would last a hundred years after we have gone. Why not think big and leave a mark for those who follow? That is the true measure of value.

Success Is...

Success is understanding that wealth is not a thing, it is a thought.

Money is minted personality. People who have it usually have an entirely different mindset from those who do not.
The basic necessities of life, food and shelter, are met early as those with a strong mindset look toward bigger and brighter horizons.

Success Is...

Success is understanding the
cost and benefit ratio.

Every benefit has a cost, but not every cost has a benefit. Sometimes we spend enormous amounts of energy and money toward goals that do not have a benefit for anyone. Make sure that there is a benefit for every cost. Otherwise, you are wasting large portions of your life and will only be met with disappointment.

Success is not allowing the
world to cookie-cut you.

Most people feel comfortable with others
who look, sound, walk, and behave like
themselves. Thus, they endeavor to make
everyone the same.
Cookie cutters are rigid and inflexible.
Cookie cutters cut out everyone the
same size.
Cookie cutters have a predetermined pattern.
Break away from the cookie cutter syndrome.
Be unique and allow God to use you in a
unique way.

Success Is...

Success is preparing to accept immediate deprivation in exchange for future gratification.

Success is not always immediate.
Sometimes it takes years to become
successful in a chosen field. Long years of
deprivation are often required to obtain
future success. Be prepared to persevere
today in order to receive success
tomorrow.

Success Is...

Success is keeping your eyes on results. Losers are always looking for excuses.

Unsuccessful people never look past the cost, the disciplines, or the possible loss when trying to make headway in life. Winners keep their eye on the results and are prepared to pay the price, take the risk, and enjoy the benefits.

Success Is...

Success is realizing that
loneliness is a part of
leadership.

Leadership is always balanced in the latitude of loneliness — loneliness because of misunderstanding, loneliness because others do not think on the same wave-length, loneliness because of the envy of others. Success in any field is usually accompanied by loneliness.

Success Is...

Success is understanding that
the mission is the ethics and
mechanics of the journey.

While focusing on a long-term goal, we tend to forget that we need a mission to reach that goal. The mission is the morality and the working commitment to the journey. Without it, you'll never reach the goal.

Success Is...

Success is being mentally
accurate and objectionably
urgent in all your deliberations.

The higher echelons of life are not achieved by a lucky break or by chance, but are pursued and obtained by those who are alert, capable, and energetic.

Success Is...

Success is recognizing the
strengths and weaknesses of
your personality.

Conduct a simple personal analysis on your strengths and your weaknesses. Have your closest friend judge its accuracy. Work on your weaknesses to make them stronger and use your strengths to do better.

Success Is...

Success is seeing the dynamic
response of setting and
achieving goals.

1. Define your goal.
2. Compose a mission statement.
3. Plan for your problems.
4. Build in reserves.
5. Relate everything to time frames.
6. Create a workable master plan to get the job done.
7. Put it into action immediately.

Success is using every moment
of time. Do not allow waiting
time to be wasted time.

When you are in a difficult situation, the natural thing to do is to wait until the crisis is over before preparing for the future. Do the opposite. Prepare for the future while your brain juices are percolating, rather than waiting for your brain to slow down to the rest position.

Success is adaptation to change.

There is nothing as permanent as change. Being able to benefit from changing circumstances ensures success. Very often it is better to change with the circumstances, rather than try to change the circumstances.

Success Is...

Success is understanding that if you are not moving ahead, you are going backwards.

The status quo is no place for the person aspiring to success. Even while waiting you can be growing, learning, and preparing for the future. The biggest challenge mankind has is coming to grips with the confusion and contradictions from within.

Success Is...

Success is understanding that faith turns weaknesses into strengths.

The Bible says faith is the substance of things hoped for and the evidence of things not seen. Faith in God always gives confidence and strength in times of trouble. It also provides a moral compass when facing uncertainty.

Success Is...

Success is knowing your exit options.

In any endeavor, remember that there are further opportunities down the road. Always have your exit options planned in case you want to move on to something that is more challenging.

Success Is...

Success is understanding that entrepreneurs are the lifeblood of a country.

A government makes a country great by providing laws that entrepreneurs can work within. It is the entrepreneurial spirit that, when fully developed, gives a country greatness and prosperity by lifting the living standard of its people. So why don't you become one of this rare breed?

Success Is...

Success is having a sense of grandeur towards life.

Consider your life a great gift from God to do, to create, and to be all that you want to be. God never intended you to be a robot and is committed to your development. Grasp life with both hands and give it all you've got.